PANZERS IN THE BALKANS AND ITALY

Early model PzKpfw VAs without ball-mount hull machine-guns
(478/3164/39).

BRUCE QUARRIE
PANZERS IN THE BALKANS AND ITALY

WORLD WAR 2 PHOTO ALBUM NUMBER 19

A selection of German wartime photographs
from the Bundesarchiv, Koblenz

PSL **Patrick Stephens, Cambridge**

First published in 1981

British Library Cataloguing in Publication Data

Panzers in the Balkans and Italy.– (World War 2
    photo albums; no. 19)
    1. Germany. Heer – Armored troops – History
    – Pictorial works   2. World War, 1939–1945 –
    Campaigns – Balkan Peninsula – Pictorial works
    3. World War, 1939–1945 – Campaigns – Italy –
    Pictorial works   4. World War, 1939–1945 –
    Tank warfare – Pictorial works
    I. Quarrie, Bruce   II. Series
    940.54′21   D757.54

    ISBN 0 85059 456 1 (casebound)
    ISBN 0 85059 457 X (softbound)

Photoset in 10pt Plantin Roman. Printed in Great
Britain on 100 gsm Fineblade coated cartridge and
bound by The Garden City Press Limited,
Letchworth, Hertfordshire SG6 1JS, for the
publishers, Patrick Stephens Limited, Bar Hill,
Cambridge, CB3 8EL, England.

CONTENTS

Acknowledgements
The author and publisher would like to express their sincere thanks to Mrs Marianne Loenartz of the Bundesarchiv for her assistance, without which this book would have been impossible.

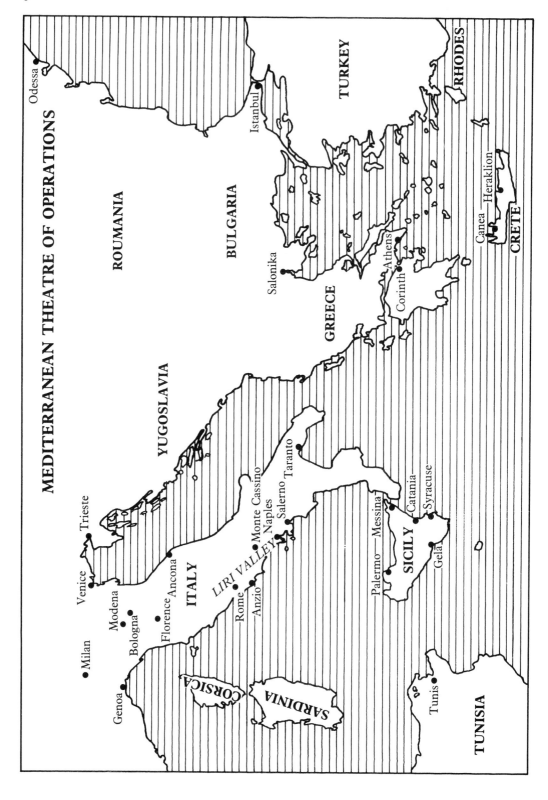

MEDITERRANEAN THEATRE OF OPERATIONS

Hitler's involvement in the Balkans was a military mistake almost, although not quite, as bad as Napoleon's 'Spanish ulcer'. It became, essentially, a police action against partisans, sapping manpower and resources which were badly needed elsewhere.

Shortly after Mussolini had declared war on France and England in June 1940 (while German troops were crossing the Seine!), the Italian dictator turned on Greece. Having successfully annexed Albania in April 1939, he now accused the Greek Government of having a non-neutral attitude and demanded that it renounce England's guarantee of independence. During August and September 1940 over 40,000 Italian troops were amassed along the border between Albania and Greece, and on October 28 Mussolini handed the Greek Government a list of 'grievances' together with a demand that Italian troops should be allowed into the country.

Italian forces began to move into Greece before a reply had even been received to this ultimatum and, on October 31, British troops began landing. The Italians fared no better on the land than they were already doing at sea. The Greek Army mobilised rapidly and switched to the offensive, trapping 5,000 crack Italian Alpine troops in the Pindus Gorge and, during November, actually pushing into Albania itself. By the end of 1940, nearly a quarter of Albania was in Greek control.

It rapidly became apparent that reluctant German participation in the Italian fiasco here – as in North Africa – was only a matter of time; indeed, the principal reason the Greek Government had not hitherto requested the assistance of the full British Expeditionary Force had been to try to avoid provoking Hitler into intervening. So, in late February 1941, the first elements of a combined Anglo-Australian-New Zealand force began landing from Egypt.

In his book *Panzer Battles* (Cassell, 1955),

General-Major F. W. von Mellenthin relates just how unwelcome these Balkan developments were to the German High Command, particularly since they placed the vital German-controlled oilfields at Ploesti, in Rumania, within reach of RAF bombers. Intervention in the Balkans would also delay Hitler's invasion of Russia and this has often been proposed as one of the reasons why the Germans failed to capture Moscow in the autumn of 1941.

German forces began assembling in Rumania in January 1941 and moved into Bulgaria in March after Hitler had forced the Bulgarian Government to join the Tripartite Pact on the 1st of that month. This put obvious strategic pressure on Yugoslavia, whose borders had become untenable as a result, and on March 20 Prince Paul's government also decided to join the Pact. For once, however, matters did not proceed in the German favour for, a week later, a coup d'état by General Simović overthrew the Yugoslav Government and replaced it by an anti-Nazi regime in the name of King Peter. Hitler retaliated with Directive No 25 ordering the destruction of Yugoslavia as well as Greece.

The operation against Yugoslavia, which involved the 5th, 8th, 9th, 11th and 14th Panzer Divisions, with the 16th held in reserve, as well as the 2nd SS Division 'Reich', was a virtual walkover since the country was divided into so many different ethnic groups, including the pro-German Croats and others of German or Italian extraction and sympathy. Simović only succeeded in mobilising two-thirds of his 31 divisions (three of which were cavalry and none of which included any armour), and the Croatian troops surrendered in droves at the first opportunity.

(Many Moslem Croatians later joined the Waffen-SS in order to fight against Tito's Christian Serbian guerrillas; the 13th Waffen Gebirgs Division 'Handschar-Kroatische' Nr 1 being formed under Brigadeführer Sauberzweig in summer 1943. This unit attained a poor fighting reputation but a notoriety for atrocities against civilians. Yugoslav Germans formed the nucleus for the 7th SS Freiwilligen Gebirgs Division 'Prinz Eugen' under Gruppenführer Phelps in spring 1942, a tougher fighting formation but one, again, with an unenviable reputation for cruelty.)

General von Weichs' II Army moved south from Austria, supported by the 46

Panzer Korps pushing south-east from Hungary then down towards Belgrade, and Panzer Group Kleist heading north-west to meet them from Bulgaria; while in the south XII Army moved simultaneously southwards into Greece from Bulgaria and west to link up with Italian troops in Albania.

As more than one commentator has observed, the Yugoslav campaign was 'more like a peacetime exercise than a bloody operation of war'. XII Army began operations on April 6 and entered Skopje on the 10th, when part of its forces were detached to help the Italians and the remainder swept victoriously into Greece. II Army did not begin moving until the 8th, heading towards Zagreb, while the two Panzer Groups formed a pincer movement aimed at Belgrade, which was first entered by a reconnaissance unit of the 2nd SS Division 'Reich' attached to 46 Panzer Korps, although 11th Panzer Division later claimed this distinction. In any case, the 'race' was very close. Belgrade fell on the 12th and the last organised Yugoslav resistance, in Sarajevo, was crushed the following day. The German troops were hailed as liberators practically everywhere, and General Simović resigned on the 14th, the armistice being signed in Prince Paul's castle on the 17th.

In Greece the resistance was both tougher and better organised, even though the end was never in question. Against XII Army's ten divisions, including the 2nd Panzer Division, the Greeks could muster only $7\frac{1}{2}$ in the front line, supported by the 2nd New Zealand and 6th Australian Divisions and a British armoured brigade, all commanded by General Maitland Wilson. Two Greek divisions were covering the deployment of the Commonwealth forces, two were in the gap between the rivers Vardar and Struma, while the remainder occupied the Metaxas Line between the Struma and the Turkish border. The remainder of the Greek Army – another 14 divisions – was still engaged with the Italians in Albania.

The Metaxas Line was not defended in sufficient strength to stand a chance of holding out. XII Army began moving on April 6 and had breached the line within 24 hours, opening the road to Salonika and the rear of the other Greek dispositions. Three days later those elements of XII Army which had invaded Serbia were also across the border and, on the 13th, Greek forces began withdrawing from Albania – but too late, for they

were now cut off. This left the Commonwealth forces holding the line of the River Aliakmon in an untenable position, and on the 16th Maitland Wilson gave the order to begin withdrawing towards the Thermopylae Line.

The 2nd Panzer Division and 6th Gebirgsjäger Division were ordered to try to stop the retreat by means of an outflanking manoeuvre around Mount Olympus. 2nd Panzer Division was split into two battlegroups advancing through the extremely difficult terrain either side of the mountain, while the alpine troops moved straight through the centre. A forced night march by the eastern battlegroup brought the Germans into the flank and rear of the New Zealand battalion holding the coastal high ground and forced them to retire in haste, abandoning much of their equipment. Two companies of tanks were laboriously brought up and forded the torrent of the River Pinios – although not without mishap – giving them access to the southern bank and the Australian forces holding the Tempe Gorge, guarding the approach to Larissa. The Australians were already under pressure from 6th Gebirgsjäger Division and the western battlegroup of 2nd Panzer Division and, lacking anti-tank guns in sufficient quantity, the Australians were forced to retreat. Larissa fell to the Germans on the 19th.

The retiring Commonwealth forces continued to fight a series of valiant rearguard actions, making the best possible use of the terrain, and even German officers on the spot acknowledged that this phase of the operations was conducted with skill. At Thermopylae itself a whole Panzer company was decimated by accurate close-range fire and, although the Germans made an audacious parachute drop on the Corinth Canal to try to trap the retreating troops (see *World War 2 Photo Album 7: German Paratroops in the Med*), Maitland Wilson succeeded in extricating 43,000 men from Attica and the Peloponessus. Further Greek resistance became pointless and the government capitulated on April 23.

For the remainder of the war operations in the Balkans were principally of an antiguerrilla nature in which tanks, due to the rugged character of the countryside in both Greece and Yugoslavia, were of little use. These duties were principally carried out by the 7th SS Freiwilligen Gebirgs Division 'Prinz Eugen' utilising a diverse mixture of captured and obsolete equipment. The 8th SS Kavallerie Division 'Florian Geyer' was also used in this role for a period during 1942, together with the Croatian Legion mentioned earlier.

However, the whole area continued to exercise a peculiar fascination in the mind of Hitler. After the fall of Tunisia in 1943 *and* the Allied invasion of Sicily in July of that year, the German dictator remained convinced that Greece was going to be the centre of the Allied assault on southern Europe, and eventually maintained no fewer than 20 divisions *in situ* to meet this imagined threat.

The German Army staff was more practically minded and realised that the landings in Sicily and, later, in mainland Italy, represented the real offensive. However, it was not until late in 1944, when Bulgaria – under Soviet pressure – changed sides, that Hitler permitted the withdrawal of German forces from the Greek islands. The belatedness of this action stranded over 20,000 German troops in tactically hopeless and strategically useless positions.

Similarly, the German forces in Italy suffered from Hitler's preoccupation with the Balkans. Prior to the Sicilian landings, there were only four divisions in residence, although this later grew sixfold. However, the nature of the terrain, coupled with Allied aerial supremacy, denied the Panzer divisions their proper function. In fact, the only Panzer division in 'permanent' residence was the 26th, which had been formed in October 1942 from the 23rd Infantry Division under command of General-leutnant Smilo Freiherr von Lüttwitz. Others which participated in the campaign were the 16th (which had been reformed in France after the parent unit was wiped out at Stalingrad) from June to November 1943; the 24th, briefly, from August to October of the same year; and the Luftwaffe's elite 'Hermann Göring' Division (for further details of which see my Osprey/Vanguard title *Fallschirm-panzerdivision 'Hermann Göring'*). Other formations which contained an armoured element and saw action in Italy included the 16th SS Panzer-Grenadier Division 'Reichsführer SS' and the 3rd, 15th, 29th and 90th Panzer-Grenadier Divisions.

Allied operations against the European mainland commenced with the combined amphibious/airborne assault on Sicily in July 1943 when eight divisions successfully disembarked on the island. Command of the Axis forces was divided and the German troops present were subordinate to the Italians. Although they fought as stubbornly as elsewhere, they were outnumbered and, when Italian troops in the line broke, this, coupled with an Allied outflanking manoeuvre, compelled a withdrawal to the toe of Italy across the Straits of Messina.

This defeat heralded the collapse of the Italian Fascist Government and the replacement of Mussolini by Marshal Badoglio, who immediately commenced surrender negotiations. A secret treaty was signed on September 3 at the same time that Allied troops were landing at Reggio. However, the German troops (under the command of Kesselring in the south and Rommel in the north) were prepared for such an eventuality and, when the news became public on the 8th – the day before the Allies landed at Salerno – German troops moved in to disarm the Italians and take over key positions.

However, Kesselring's position in the south was fraught as he could only dispose seven divisions, although reinforcements were on the way. Nevertheless, General Mark Clark and the US 5th Army met with extremely stiff opposition at Salerno and for the first two days of the battle it seemed as though the American troops would be thrown back into the sea. Aerial superiority won the day, though, and by the 15th the beachhead was consolidated. Meanwhile, the British 8th Army advancing up from Calabria had encountered little resistance and joined up with the Americans on the 16th.

German forces in the area now numbered 15 divisions, however, and, from the time the Allies had captured Bari and Foggia and reached the line of the River Biferno at the end of the month, they found the going far less easy. The lie of the land favoured the defenders and, with the exception of the Anzio (Nettuno) campaign, the remainder of the war in Italy settled down to become predominantly an infantry slogging match.

In this type of warfare, where mobility was secondary to concealment and firepower, the tank was really a luxury since self-propelled guns firing from prepared positions were just as effective. Indeed, many Panther tank turrets were mounted on buried casements as anti-tank 'pillboxes'. Local Allied air supremacy (it was never as complete as many people believe) severely inhibited the movement of German columns except by night.

But when they could be brought into the right place at the right time, the German Panzers could still wreak havoc, as they were to show at Anzio.

By the end of 1943 Allied forces in Italy were facing a virtual stalemate situation, and all hopes of being in Rome by Christmas had faded before the end of November. A new amphibious assault was therefore launched in January 1944 to outflank the German lines and open the coast road. This involved 50,000 American and British troops under Major-General Lucas.

The landing was virtually unopposed but, with memories of Salerno fresh in his mind, Lucas suspected a German trap and, rather than pushing boldly forward, paused to consolidate his beachhead. This gave Kesselring time to reinforce the Anzio perimeter with eight divisions, including the elite 'Hermann Göring' formation, which easily administered a check to Lucas' troops when he eventually began moving out.

Meanwhile, the Allies were having no more success in breaking through the main German defensive line, since the obvious avenue of approach up the Liri Valley was closed by the heroic Fallschirmjägers and other defenders of Monte Cassino. After two determined assaults had proved fruitless in results and costly in lives, the Allies brought in the air force to bomb the monastery. However, this only succeeded in making it even more impregnable and a third attack proved equally futile.

During February General Clark visited the Anzio beachhead and organised a breakout attempt – which proved similarly fruitless and provoked a German counter-attack which almost drove the Americans back to the beaches. Heavy naval gunfire saved the day for the Allies, however, and the German forces were obliged to fall back.

The stalemate continued for two months, Allied operations being particularly hampered by heavy rains but, on May 11 a renewed attack on Cassino, preceded by a 2,000-gun artillery barrage, succeeded in dislodging the exhausted and depleted defenders. At the same time a renewed attack was mounted out of the Anzio beachhead and, since Kesselring was unable adequately to reinforce either position in time, the road to Rome finally lay open. Kesselring declared Rome an open city on June 4 to prevent it being bombed and withdrew his forces to the Gothic Line 150 miles to the north. Allied troops in Italy were thus able to celebrate the news of D-Day two days later with their own victory.

However, events elsewhere now took a hand as many of General Alexander's troops were withdrawn from Italy to take part in Operation 'Dragoon' – the invasion of southern France – so that, despite local successes such as the capture of Ancono and Livorno, Kesselring's tired but stubborn troops were given time to settle into their new dispositions. Alexander, together with General Clark and Prime Minister Churchill, were angry and frustrated by this diversion of valuable troops at a critical time and were unable properly to exploit a breach in the Gothic Line at Lake Trasimene. The offensive did not gather way again until September when, however, three successive breaches were opened, despite heavy casualties, in the German line.

Under pressure from all sides, Hitler finally realised that his forces were overstretched and at long last, as mentioned earlier, agreed to a partial withdrawal of German troops in Greece. British paratroops followed up the advantage and, on October 16, the Greek Government-in-exile returned to Athens. In Italy, however, with the aid of reinforcements and the heavy rains which again hampered the Allies, Kesselring managed to staunch the breaches in the Gothic Line and the situation reverted to stalemate.

The situation remained much the same until April 1945, although on the German side Field Marshal Kesselring was wounded and yielded command to von Vietinghoff. (Kesselring was committed to life imprisonment by a war crimes tribunal but later pardoned and released in 1952). The Allies secured local victories such as the capture of Ravenna in December 1944 but concentrated on preparing for a new spring offensive, relying in the intervening time on strategic bombing in this theatre.

The final offensive opened on April 9 when the British 8th Army practically decimated the troops opposing them and crossed the River Senio while, a few days later, the American 5th Army finally succeeded in capturing Bologna. With the Russians in Berlin and the Allied troops everywhere else victorious, the morale of the surviving German troops in Italy was understandably at an all-time ebb and, harried by Italian partisans, the retreating men began throwing down their arms at an ever increasing rate. As

American troops entered Milan on the 29th Hitler committed suicide and the German troops in Italy surrendered unconditionally.

The men on each side had fought a particularly difficult war in Italy leading to frustrations and a degree of atrocity – such as the shooting of prisoners – by both. The Germans suffered particularly from the depradations of partisans, making the life of rear-echelon troops particularly nervewracking and even the occasional leave for front-line soldiers a far from relaxing experience. On their part, the Allied troops were up against seasoned defenders in strong and well-camouflaged positions which also afforded them a greater degree of protection from the elements.

The conduct of the campaign has often been questioned and the doggedness of the German defence is usually attributed solely to Hitler's fanatical resistance to giving up an inch of ground. As Kesselring himself said, however, in his *Memoirs* (William Kimber, 1953), 'To evacuate the whole of Italy and defend the Reich from positions in the Alps . . . would have given the enemy untrammelled freedom of movement in the direction of France and the Balkans, have meant sacrificing an indispensable deep battle-zone and unleashing the air war on the whole of southern Germany and Austria'. Interested readers may find a deeper analysis of this question – particularly Hitler's interference and the problems of a divided German command at the time of the Salerno landings – in Matthew Cooper's fine book *The German Army 1933–1945* (Macdonald and Jane's, 1978).

In closing this, the last title of mine in this series, I would like to sincerely acknowledge the helpful comments, criticisms and suggestions of the many readers who have taken the trouble to write to me. This has enabled many gaps and some errors in photo identification and interpretation to be rectified, and hopefully in the fullness of time these will be incorporated in future revised editions of the books (Nos 1 to 4 are already available).

The photographs in this book have been selected with care from the Bundesarchiv, Koblenz (the approximate German equivalent of the US National Archives or the British Public Records Office). Particular attention has been devoted to choosing photographs which will be fresh to the majority of readers, although it is inevitable that one or two may be familiar. Other than this, the author's prime concern has been to choose good-quality photographs which illustrate the type of detail that enthusiasts and modellers require. In certain instances quality has, to a degree, been sacrificed in order to include a particularly interesting photograph. For the most part, however, the quality speaks for itself.

The Bundesarchiv files hold some one million black and white negatives of Wehrmacht and Luftwaffe subjects, including 150,000 on the Kriegsmarine, some 20,000 glass negatives from the inter-war period and several hundred colour photographs. Sheer numbers is one of the problems which makes the compilation of a book such as this difficult. Other difficulties include the fact that, in the vast majority of cases, the negatives have not been printed so the researcher is forced to look through box after box of 35 mm contact strips – some 250 boxes containing an average of over 5,000 pictures each, plus folders containing a further 115,000 contact prints of the Waffen-SS; moreover, cataloguing and indexing the negatives is neither an easy nor a short task, with the result that, at the present time, Luftwaffe and Wehrmacht subjects as well as entirely separate theatres of operations are intermingled in the same files.

There is a simple explanation for this confusion. The Bundesarchiv photographs were taken by war correspondents attached to German military units, and the negatives were originally stored in the Reich Propaganda Ministry in Berlin. Towards the close of World War 2, all the photographs – then numbering some $3\frac{1}{2}$ million – were ordered to be destroyed. One man in the Ministry, a Herr Evers, realised that they should be preserved for posterity and, acting entirely unofficially and on his own initiative, commandeered the first available suitable transport – two refrigerated fish trucks – loaded the negatives into them, and set out for safety. Unfortunately, one of the trucks disappeared en route and, to this day, nobody knows what happened to it. The remainder were captured by the Americans and shipped to Washington, where they remained for 20 years before the majority were returned to the government of West Germany. A large number, however, still reside in Washington. Thus the Bundesarchiv files are incomplete, with infuriating gaps for any researcher. Specifically, they end in the autumn of 1944, after Arnhem, and thus record none of the drama of the closing months of the war.

The photographs are currently housed in a modern office block in Koblenz, overlooking the River Mosel. The priceless negatives are stored in the basement, and there are strict security checks on anyone seeking admission to the Bildarchiv (Photo Archive). Regretably, and the author has been asked to stress this point, the archives are *only open to bona fide authors and publishers, and prints can only be supplied for reproduction in a book or magazine.* They CANNOT be supplied to private collectors or enthusiasts for personal use, so *please* – don't write to the Bundesarchiv or the publishers of this book asking for copy prints, because they cannot be provided. The well-equipped photo laboratory at the Bundesarchiv is only capable of handling some 80 to 100 prints per day because each is printed individually under strictly controlled conditions – another reason for the fine quality of the photographs but also a contributory factor in the above legislation.

Right Early PzKpfw VAs in Rome being photographed by an SS officer (716/11/8).

THE PHOTOGRAPHS

14

Above Crossing the border—probably into Yugoslavia—through a rather flimsy anti-tank barrier (161/209/26).

Left and facing page PzKpfw IIIHs of the 5th Panzer Division en route to the Balkans (158/94/11, 12 and 13).

OVERLEAF
Background photograph PzKpfw IIIF of the 5th Panzer Division in Yugoslavia (159/107/36).

Inset left PzBefWg IIIH of the 5th Panzer Division (159/107/37).

Inset right Another 5th Panzer Division PzKpfw IIIH (159/144/28).

Left PzKpfw IVC of the 5th Panzer Division (159/144/15).

Below and facing page During the invasions of Yugoslavia and Greece, the Panzer divisions had to use 'roads' wherever they could find them, as in the case of this 5th Division PzKpfw II **(below)** and IIIH **(right)** (162/294/9a and 11a), or **(below right)** these IIIHs (162/293/27a).

Above A dodgy river crossing for another PzKpfw III (162/256/39).

Below 11th Panzer Division PzKpfw IIIF (161/215/11).

This page The difficulty experienced by tanks in the Yugoslav and Greek mountains can clearly be seen in these shots of PzKpfw IIIs, heavily laden with spare kit (166/515/10 and 22).

Left PzKpfw IVs, probably of the 11th Panzer Division, in the Balkans (161/247/29a).

Below Panzer crewmen clear away barbed wire in front of a PzKpfw IIIF (166/515/24).

Right PzKpfw IIIs in Greece; background vehicle is an Ausf F with old-style commander's cupola and driver's visor, while that in the foreground is a late Ausf G or an H (162/257/12a).

Below right A German motor-cyclist examines a knocked-out British Cruiser Tank Mark IIA (A10) nicknamed 'Connie II' in Greece (163/316/37).

This and facing page 5th Panzer Division armoured cars in Greece: an SdKfz 232 ('Seydlitz') **(above)**, 233 ('Panther') **(below)** and 221 ('Houx') **(right)** (163/327/24, 175/1265/14 and 164/369/29a).

Left And who said battle re-enactments were a post-war phenomenon? Self-conscious German troops with cardboard armour and shields (but note their boots!) put on a carnival for the 'locals' (167/562/2).

Below left and this page Scenes from later in the war—PzKpfw IVF2s in Athens (175/1270/25, 175/1267/23 and 175/1270/33).

These pages PzKpfw VAs in Italy (478/2164/27, 37 and 35).

This page PzKpfw IVGs entrained to—or from?—the front (175/1269/8 and 12).

Right Regrettably, the German censor has been at the back of this SdKfz 251 loaded on a train, but it was probably photographed in Greece (166/547/2).

Below right and overleaf PzKpfw IIAs, Bs and Cs of the 9th Panzer Division in the Balkans (160/190/34, 160/152/32, 160/190/29 and 38).

Right Early PzKpfw IIIG with 3.7 cm KwK L/46.5 and internal mantlet. Only about 50 Ausführung Gs were so armed (160/190/28).

Below 9th Panzer Division PzKpfw IIIG (160/190/33).

Left Well-laden PzKpfw IIIG of the 9th Panzer Division (157/21/23a).

Below After the fall of France, large numbers of French AFVs were pressed into German service, normally for second-line and anti-partisan duties. Here a smoke grenade partially obscures a Hotchkiss H-39 during an exercise or demonstration (206/1857/20).

Right Unidentified insignia on the rear of another H-39 (173/1143/23).

Below right A Hotchkiss H-38 which has come to grief. The Germans replaced the domed cupolas on French tanks with the split-hatch type seen here (174/1152/14).

Left A Renault R-35 in German service (174/1153/28).

Below A Hotchkiss H-39 in bleak conditions (173/1101/33).

Right An H-39 in the Yugoslav mountains (172/1092/33a).

Below right A Somua S-35 in the Balkans. Until the appearance of the Russian T-34, a good case could be made for rating this the best tank in service anywhere (169/948/11).

Facing page A Hotchkiss H-39 '323' with an infantry patrol in a Balkan forest (169/916/18 and 23a).

Above '334' photographed at the same time (169/917/2).

Below Although probably taken in Russia rather than the Balkans, this picture of an H-39 will be of interest to modellers because of the 'hut on skis' which it is towing! (168/880/15).

Left Track repairs for a Somua S-35 in Greece (169/915/21).

Above A convoy of PzKpfw IBs crossing a wooden bridge. Although obsolete even before 1941, this vehicle continued in service until 1943 (157/41/8).

Below PzKpfw IVG (479/2196/19a).

This page A well-camouflaged Panther. Note zimmerit on turret (477/2124/4 and 6).

This page Heavily covered with foliage, a convoy of Nashorns passes through an Italian town (316/1161/20 and 21).

Above left Another Nashorn, revealing rather
more of itself! Of interest are the lengths of wire
criss-crossing the superstructure into which fresh
foliage could be inserted for camouflage
(313/1004/9a).

Far left, left and this page Good detail views of
PzKpfw VAs with new style cupola but lacking
the ball-mounted hull machine-gun later fitted to
this mark of Panther (478/2165/16 and 18,
2166/18a and 37).

Above left The Brumbaer was a self-propelled gun on the PzKpfw IV chassis designed for infantry support in street fighting and against fortifications. Mounting a 15 cm howitzer, this vehicle was issued to Sturmpanzer Abteilungs 217, 218 and 219 in Italy (313/1004/5a).

Left As only 52 vehicles were converted, photographs of the Brumbaer are comparatively rare. Here a column of British prisoners marches past one which is preceded by a PzKpfw II. Italy, autumn 1943 (310/900/31).

Above The zimmerit coating for protection against magnetic mines is very clear in this shot (311/904/7a).

Right A Brumbaer at speed along an Italian road (312/955/4a).

Above left An improvised tank-killer. A captured Carden-Loyd carrier with Horstmann suspension in the hands of the 3rd Panzer-Grenadier Division in Italy. The three Racketenpanzerbüchse 43 8.8 cm rocket launchers must have been a formidable combination at close range (313/1003/3).

Left A knocked-out Sherman among the burnt-out wreckage of another vehicle in Italy, 1944 (313/1004/25a).

This page Sherman used for target practice well illustrating the armour-piercing capability of the 5 cm KwK39 L/60, the 7.5 cm KwK42 L/70 and the 8.8 cm KwK36 L/56 (313/1004/20 and 21).

Left The mud in Italy could be every bit as bad as in Russia! Here a Wespe has apparently just been towed out by an SdKfz 9/1, an 18-ton half-track mounting a 6-ton crane. In the left foreground is an Italian M13/40 (312/968/20).

Below left Tank crewmen, wearing the late-war denims, with captured Allied Shermans (311/944/6a).

Right A barrel change for a Nashorn courtesy of a 6-ton crane mounted on a four-wheeled truck (311/908/23).

Below A Panzer crewman contemplates with despondency the task of refitting this Tiger's track (311/904/23a).

Background photograph and overleaf top Uncaring traffic rumbles past a Tiger stranded in a ditch (311/903/22 and 25).

Inset A veteran Panzer Feldwebel (311/904/14a).

Below More Tiger track repairs in an Italian orchard (311/904/10).

Facing page Shedding a track seems to have been an occupational hazard for Tiger crews! (310/898/25, 899/16a and 19a).

Above A disabled Goliath remote-controlled demolition tank (310/898/34).

Below StuG III in Italy (310/896/6).

Right A clear shot of a Tiger, autumn 1943 (?) (310/880/27).

Above 'Ellzapoppin II' and another Sherman after a confrontation with the German Panzers (310/876/23).

Below Following the Italian surrender, a great deal of equipment was taken over by the German forces, including this Autoblinda AB41 armoured car (309/820/16).

Above Even in defeat, the Wehrmacht retained a sense of humour . . . but I would love to know the story behind this picture **(above left)** (305/674/30), or **(above right)** this equally silly shot of an 11th Panzer Division car! (163/303/30a).

Below 20 mm Flak 38 mounted on a light half-track (306/713/20).

Above Rare close-up of a PzKpfw III (Fl) flamethrower tank (306/730/24).

Below The crew of a PzKpfw IVE bargain for fresh fruit with a Greek or Yugoslav farmer (307/762/8a).

Above Panthers roll into action, Italy 1943 (478/2167/31).

Below PzKpfw IV crests a ridge on a mountain road (308/799Q/19a).

These pages and overleaf PzKpfw IVGs of the 16th Panzer Division (305/652/13, 14, 16, 22 and 24).

Above Setting up a Nebelwerfer in an Italian field (304/643/15).

Below SdKfz 231 in Italy (304/634/26a).

Captured M-10 in German service (304/626/12a).

These pages Hiding a PzKpfw VA (early model with 'letterbox' machine-gun flap instead of later ball-mount) in an Italian village (313/1001/17, 27, 32 and 35).

These pages 7.5 cm Pak 40s in action in Italy (304/614/20 and 615/30).

Above left A moment's relaxation for the crew of a well-camouflaged '88' (304/626/5a).

Left Despite the poor quality of this photo, it is a particularly interesting shot as it shows one of the little CV33s produced with torsion bar suspension principally for export to Brazil, here in Fallschirmjäger hands in Italy (304/608/7).

Above Another Italian tank in German service, this time an M13/40 (304/614/7).

Right StuG III in south Italy (303/587/17a).

Above 20 mm Flakvierling—a very effective weapon against both low-flying aircraft and 'soft' ground targets (303/586/26).

Below and above right StuG III in the mountains (303/580/19 and 22).

Right PzKpfw IVG at speed (303/556/11).

These pages The 16th SS Division 'Reichsführer SS' was in Rome in January 1944, as shown in these photos of StuG IIIs (305/700/6, 11 and 19 and 312/992/13a).

Above PzKpfw IIIM (303/556/8).

Left SdKfz 233 (205/1800/34).

Above right Camouflaged StuG III in an Italian town (303/554/15a).

Right and next three pages PzKpfw IVGs of the 1st Panzer Division in Greece, August 1943 (175/1259/4a, 1264/8, 1266/8, 1267/30 and 36 and 1268/14a).

Another PzKpfw IVG, possibly photographed at the same time (176/1372/24).

These pages and overleaf Tigers and PzKpfw VAs in Rome. Unfortunately, none carry any identifying insignia (310/850/19a and 20a, 855/10a, 880/33, 35 and 38 and 884/15a).

This and next four pages The long retreat up the Italian peninsula. Visible are StuG IIIs, PzKpfw VAs, an Elefant and, of especial interest, a little Borgward SdKfz 301 Ladungsträger, or tracked demolition charge layer. Photographs from this sequence have often been attributed, incorrectly, to the Russian front (311/940/13, 16, 18, 15, 32, 34, 35 and 38).

Left A PzKpfw VA negotiates a stream (478/2165/2).

Below left and this page A PzKpfw VA shows its paces in Italy (477/2124/17, 22, 23 and 32).

APPENDIX

Comparison of Panzer divisions, 1941 and 1943

Throughout the war, Hitler was guilty of sublimating the strength of the German Army by creating new units whose strength, for the most part, had to come through filtering off elements of existing formations. In 1941 the number of Panzer divisions was doubled but – despite the replacement of old equipment by more modern vehicles and weapons – their combat effectiveness virtually halved.

A 1941 division comprised two Panzer regiments, each of two battalions, with one medium and two light companies to a battalion. A full-strength company had 30 tanks in theory, although 20 was closer to the truth. Many divisions, in fact, only had one tank regiment – although six had three – creating a significant imbalance, since there were also two infantry regiments, one artillery regiment, and armoured reconnaissance, anti-tank, anti-aircraft, engineer and signals battalions within the divisions.

A division averaged, therefore, 180 tanks, although 160 can be taken as a serviceable norm. By 1943, however, this had been further reduced to an average of 108 – with only one two-battalion regiment per division – while the infantry and artillery complements had increased. Admittedly, a higher proportion of the artillery in 1943 was self-propelled, but the re-allocation of resources demonstrates remarkably both the increasing strain imposed on German industry by Allied strategic bombing and the increasingly defensive nature of the war the Axis had to fight.

Due to the terrain, of course, there was less call for highly mobile armoured forces in the Balkans or Italy than in the land war's critical theatre – Russia – hence the paucity of the Wehrmacht's tank allocation in this area.

ACHTUNG! COMPLETED YOUR COLLECTION?

Other titles in the same series

No 1 Panzers in the Desert
by Bruce Quarrie

No 2 German Bombers over England
by Bryan Philpott

No 3 Waffen-SS in Russia
by Bruce Quarrie

No 4 Fighters Defending the Reich
by Bryan Philpott

No 5 Panzers in North-West Europe
by Bruce Quarrie

No 6 German Fighters over the Med
by Bryan Philpott

No 7 German Paratroops in the Med
by Bruce Quarrie

No 8 German Bombers over Russia
by Bryan Philpott

No 9 Panzers in Russia 1941–43
by Bruce Quarrie

No 10 German Fighters over England
by Bryan Philpott

No 11 U-Boats in the Atlantic
by Paul Beaver

No 12 Panzers in Russia 1943–45
by Bruce Quarrie

No 13 German Bombers over the Med
by Bryan Philpott

No 14 German Capital Ships
by Paul Beaver

No 15 German Mountain Troops
by Bruce Quarrie

No 16 German Fighters over Russia
by Bryan Philpott

No 17 E-Boats and Coastal Craft
by Paul Beaver

No 18 German Maritime Aircraft
by Bryan Philpott

No 20 German Destroyers and Escorts
by Paul Beaver

ACHTUNG! COMPLETED YOUR COLLECTION?